Peaceful
mind
GRATEFUL
Heart

YOGA
AND
COFFEE
ARE ALL I NEED

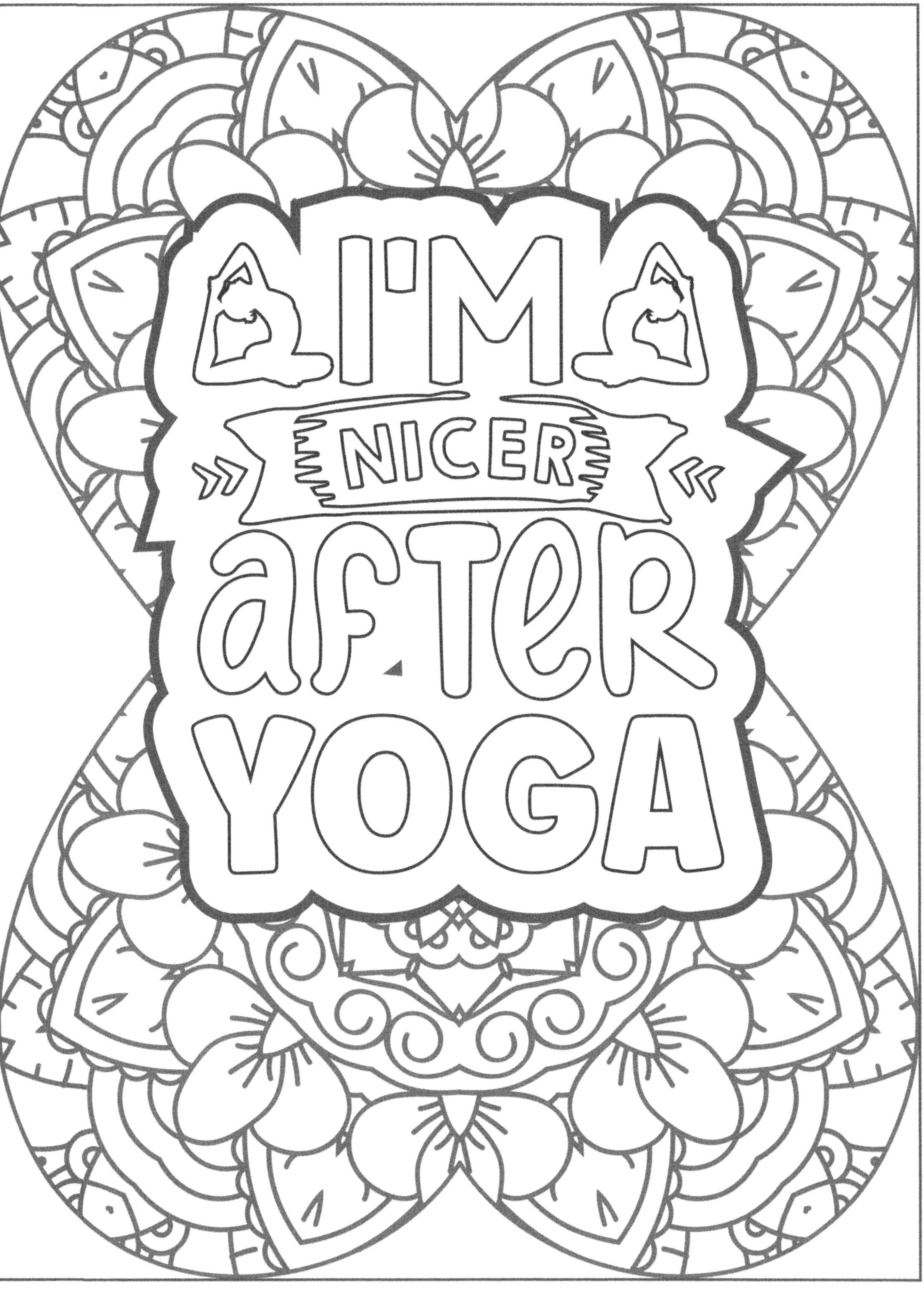
I'M
NICER
after
YOGA

YOGA
vibes
Only

INHALE
THE FUTURE
EXHALE
THE PAST

Namaste

It's
a good
D·A·Y
to start
with
YOGA

I will
Catch you
If you
~ fail ~
-Yoga Mat

SIPPIN'
ON Zen
AND
Juice

Stressed
Blessed
AND YOGA
Obsessed

Everything
i need is
WITHIN ME

FIND
YOURSELF
Be
That

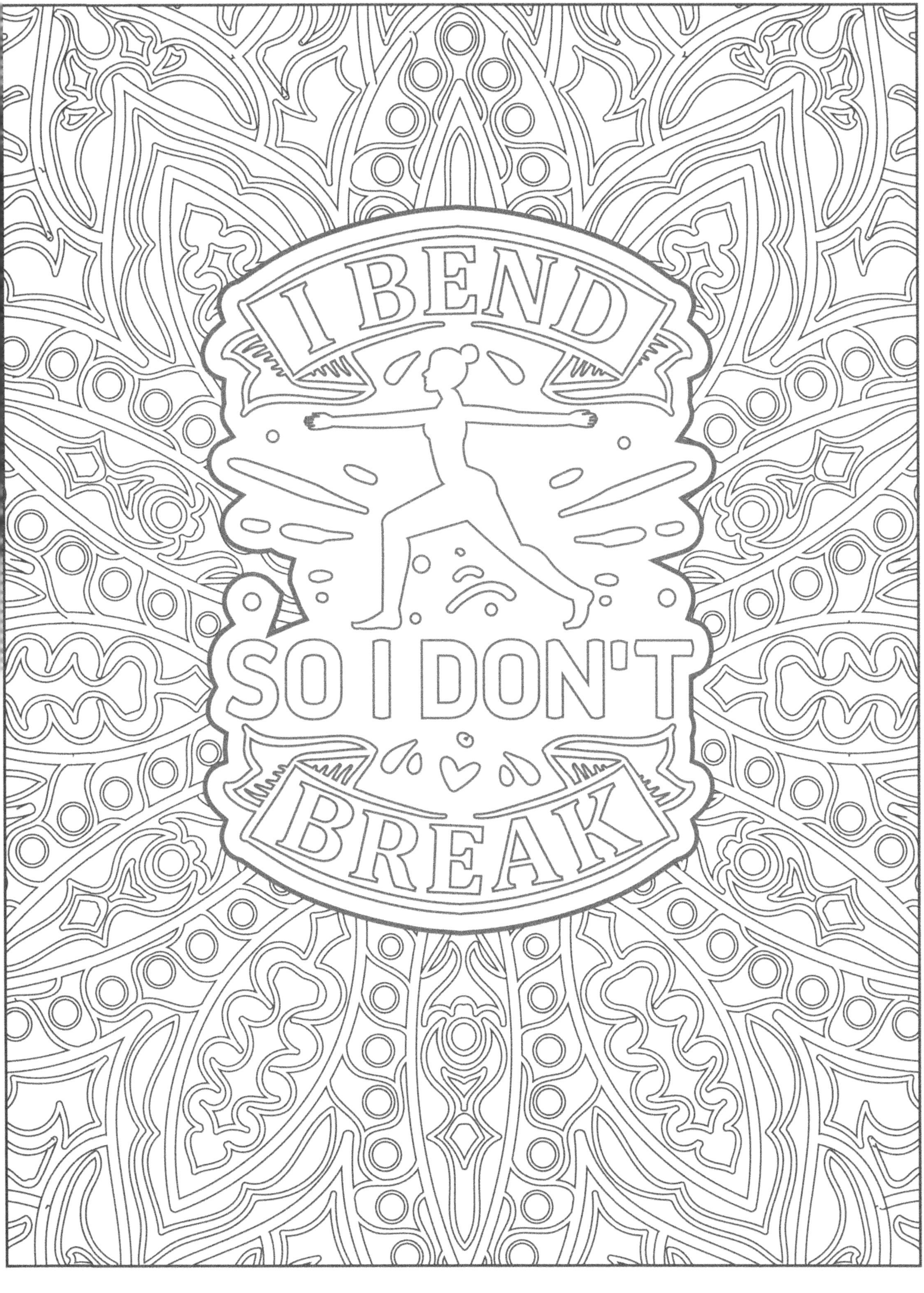
I BEND
SO I DON'T
BREAK

Pride
tribe

Yoga
Instructor
24/7

Yoga
IS THE
SCIENCE
OF
Reality

EAT.
SLEEP.
YOGA.

GO
With
THE
Flow

YOGA BRINGS
Clarity
TO
Life,
NOT
Confusion

Forget
DIAMONDS
Just Give
ME YOGA
Pants

EAT
Sleep
YOGA
REPEAT

YOGA
BECAUSE
ADULTING
is hard

I'M ONLY
Doing
THIS FOR
PIZZA

it's
YOGA
o'clock

MORE
LESS
STRETCHING
STRESSING

YOGA
Gives YOU
SUPERPOWERS

Peace
Love &
Yoga

Made in the USA
Monee, IL
21 March 2022

93263908R00037